Third Rail

Third Rail

Poems by

Beth Boylan

Cover design by Shay Culligan
Cover image by Zoe via Unsplash
Author photo by Beth Boylan

ISBN: 978-1-63980-739-0

Kelsay Books
502 South 1040 East, A-119
American Fork, Utah 84003
Kelsaybooks.com

to Emily, my sister, first reader, first co-pilot

to my parents, for their love

to Laura Cyphers's Monday night poetry group

to Dara-Lyn Shrager, transcendent poet and editor,
for her razor-sharp eye and ear, wit, and generosity of time

and to Frank O'Hara, my first and forever poet love

Acknowledgments

I am grateful to the editors and readers of the following journals, in which these poems originally appeared (in some cases, in different form):

34 Orchard: "Things We Did on the Internet"
Birdcoat Quarterly: "Insomnia"
Broadkill Review: "Dead Things"
Chronogram: "To New Paltz"
Dying Dahlia Review: "Ash Wednesday"
Gyroscope Review: "Hysterectomy," "Playing Detectives"
Jelly Bucket: "Air Conditioner"
The McNeese Review: "Prayer"
New York Quarterly: "Lines for Self"
Nixes Mate Review: "At the Lake"
Oyster River Pages: "Fireworks"
Peatsmoke: "Breakfast," "Rocks"
Remington Review: "Afternoon Storm"
Rockvale Review: "Butterfly Weed," "Cataracts"
Rust + Moth: "Arrowhead"
San Pedro Review: "Giant"
Thimble: "Third Rail"
Two Hawks Quarterly: "Grant Road," "Sins"

Contents

Grant Road

Summers at Grandma's house
my sister and I baked cakes in the sandbox,
roasted hot dogs pierced onto sticks from the brush.

Our mother poked garbage down into a barrel,
burning a fire that scorched the dusk
and left our hand-me-downs smoky for days.

I swung from the old tire and watched her
cigarette smoke spiral into the pines,
imagined ghosts playing with lightning bugs,

thought, *Run, Run.*

Ghost Apple

My brother died one night in January, when I was barely two.
I never knew he was the blond boy with dark chocolate eyes
in the photos on shelves around the house. I never understood
so many things: slamming doors and dishes, the car gunning
out of the garage and up the road, curse words, hushed words,
no words—
what made my parents flick the switch between silence and rage.
Where to escape to when they did.

I could not fathom the forbidden: Eleanor Rigby on the radio
and yellow toy cranes, the spools of brown film unraveling
behind the National Geographics in the basement.

One summer afternoon: my father mowed the dead lawn,
my mother made a pitcher of tea and spoke his name out loud:
Jimmy
After my father and his father. No more fathers now.
End of the family line with just you and your sister left.

She chopped mint leaves on the cutting board,
grabbed ice cubes from the freezer,
whispered: *loved to play   loved to hum*
fever   hospital   never came home

I didn't like this story, wanted a new one:
ran upstairs to grab my bubblegum cards for the trade,
stuffed my pinkies in my ears and hummed—

I read of a farmer once who found the icy shell of an apple hanging
from a branch in winter, its core lay crumpled on the frozen ground
below: nobody tells us how to fill the hole, tend to what remains,
what to do with the ghosts we are given.

That day I loaded up my water pistol and ran outside,
shot it up at the trees, shot it up toward the sun,
tore off my tee-shirt to bare my chest like my father's,
shouted, *See?! I can be a boy! Look at me, look at me!*

Sins

In grammar school the nuns warned us
that the nearby dam would not hold forever,
that the sins of dirty girls and boys
would one day smash the barrier
and release the reservoir's waters to drown us.
When some kids unearthed a bag of pornos
during recess one day, I figured this was it.
I stared at those glossy parts—raw, fleshy, pink, hard—
giggling in horror, waiting for the floodgates to open
as my friends played Spin the Bottle and flipped the pages,
already hooked. That night I practiced my swim strokes in bed
and prayed the Hail Mary over and over,
asking forgiveness for things I did not yet understand.
I did not wonder why a man might have buried magazines
near a playground, I did not yet know of such sins.

Air Conditioner

Back home on summer nights, my mother would plug in the
electric floor fan and tilt it toward me just so,
before going back downstairs to my father.

I would lie in the dark and listen to the metal propellers clank
over the cicadas, passing cars, and TV
muffling the shouting below.

One night I saw my grandmother standing by my bed, another
night my brother, faces blurred, arms outstretched,
pulsing flashes of violet light;

a professor once explained that she was visited by dead soldiers in
her sleep—I never knew there was a name for it.

I turned off the fan every night that one summer, convinced that
Son of Sam was creeping up the stairs, that my mother and father
were yelling to scare him into putting down his .44
or to at least leave our house.

I still fall asleep facing the door
and turn off the angry hiss of the air conditioner—
how else to hear the ghosts and madmen coming?

Emily

That summer night your throat closed, I sat
on the boulder at the edge of the driveway
and prayed to the saints I'd been taught in school.
I had yet to learn of the heart. I left you
lying there on that chocolate corduroy couch,
our mother standing stiff and still
as you gasped for breath, our neighbor
racing down the street in her housecoat to help.
Your lips purpled in the gloaming
as I counted my sins instead of stars
and whispered *I'll do better* to the Holy Ghost.
I closed my fist around a firefly
and felt something inside me crack.
I knew nothing of love until this.

Butterfly Weed

My mother used to place wildflowers in books between tissues.
When they dried, I would sit at her elbow and watch her gently
remove the flattened sprigs of Queen Anne's Lace or pansy
to arrange and frame under glass.
The summer of the drought we watched her garden die.
One afternoon on the way back from the A&P, she slammed
on the brakes and pointed off the highway. *Butterfly Weed,* she
whispered. *It's endangered.*
I couldn't get out of the car fast enough. Ran through the dead
grass that reached past my hips to snatch those flowers, hot and
orange as fire. Back in the car, my mother's lips stretched
into an *O* as I passed her the loot.
She placed them in her lap and raised dust clouds as she gunned us
back on the road.
Grabbed my hand and checked the rearview mirror.
Two outlaws on the run.
I'd never seen her so happy.

At the Wednesday Night Gay Men's Health Crisis Meetings (circa 1997, NYC)

They would waltz in, fluttering of the coming weekend
or the one just past, sharing timetables for films at the Quad
or Fire Island trains. Over tepid coffee, they'd fold open
chairs and swap T-cell counts. Drop names of the friends
they had visited that week at St. Vincent's. I sat just outside
their circle, writing down their minutes in the notebook on my lap.
One night the guest speaker was a man who'd gone blind.
He cradled his wallet as if he were holding the cure—
showed us how he'd learned to fold each bill and feel
for a 5, 10, or 20 when buying subway tokens or dumplings.
Joked that his mother would be proud that he'd taken up origami,
though they hadn't spoken in years.
Someone laughed too loudly. I doodled a broken swan.
He missed the dances on Sunday afternoons,
never left his apartment much. He wished he had more time.
When the hour was up, another volunteer helped him with his
things as the rest of us raced to the elevator and choked up relief on
the street. The boys danced off into the Chelsea dusk,
and I ran to the river, stared down the rising moon,
traced the Jersey skyline with my finger.

Third Rail

My mother texts to tell me her phone buzzed at 3 a.m., warning her
of a potential tornado, and it's only then I remember jolting awake
to the same alert. It's how we connect now. Texts of weather,
headlines—emojis to fill in the blanks. Once in a while,
I can't picture a time before this. Like after a storm when the air
turns green and the sun spins prisms, and you think to yourself,
how in God's name could I have just been afraid.

She would drive us around the reservoir and speak of its water,
deeper than houses, black as pitch. Nothing but darkness
to strangle you if you fell in. I prayed to be good.
Prayed for her to floor the gas and get it over with.
Crouched down in the backseat and braced for impact.

When Metro-North installed the third rail down in Croton Falls,
four firemen appeared at that week's morning assembly
in the gym. The Super 8 projector spun gauzy images of plastic
dummies burning on the tracks—700 electric volts hissing
and raging inside.
I pictured my mother smashing dishes in the sink, pictured
the bowl of rainbow sherbet I'd left out on the stoop
and wondered what colors would melt out of me.

Hysterectomy

This morning some men came and chopped down another one
of the large trees, leaving just a stump and shavings
in the grass, strands of vines climbing the brick wall,
clinging wildly in their search for sustenance—

like the renegade tendrils and blood vessels
that grew outside my uterus, suffocating organs and tumor
the size of a plum; they did not perish easily either,
as the surgeon snipped and cut out my withering womb.

I think of them on summer nights like this one, as I lie awake
fingering the silverfishy scars on my sweaty skin:
did they weep as they were sliced off and discarded in the bin,
did they try to creep back as I craved a newborn to suck at my
    breast

I wonder:

did the tree howl as the first ax-blow tore open her gut
did she keen for a tiny sapling to cleave to her roots?

Ode to that Nurse

who wiped me down with a warm, wet cloth
so slowly & gently
for a moment I thought I was something beautiful.
I lay there on the gurney, gutted & dazed,
not wanting the fog & fever to lift, not wanting to face
whatever wild, sexless thing the surgery had made me.
Down, down she went—
over each knobby step of my spine,
into my sweaty, blood-tinged corners,
around the tube filtering out my pinkish piss.
My shame must have scorched her hands,
but she whispered something to me then,
so quiet I could barely hear it, *Honey,* I think,
and spooned a spot of lemon ice to my lips.

Baggage

The summer after I left you, I flew straight to San Francisco,
dragged my baggage up and down the hills toward City Lights,

where a man sat on cardboard. I wondered how much he'd lost
in love, how his eyes seemed to say, *I get you.*

Like yours did, that time we climbed up through Père Lachaise
on the bleakest of mornings, crossing paths with all the other

vultures searching for Oscar Wilde covered in lipstick kisses,
flitting between Callas and Piaf, hunting and pecking for Jim.

Unfamiliar with these scoundrels, you stood in reverence anyway,
holding my book full of Post-its, watching me place a stone on

Gertrude Stein. I'm no saint. Sometimes in the dark I worry I've
been careless with love, said goodbye to things

I could have stood a while longer. Sometimes I like to imagine I
never packed my bags, never flew away, that no storm knocked the

power out in our tiny hotel room in Paris that night after the
cemetery. Only you rushing back in, drenched and laughing,

holding out the candle, baguette, and two pats of butter
you'd snatched from the kitchen.

Cataracts

I am slicing radishes when my mother phones to say
she liked the photo of my hydrangea and she will have
her cataracts removed in September. I want to say *Finally*
but bite my tongue because she and I are killing sadness
these days, working hard at joy.
I want to say so many things:
how a flower turns from pink to blue in the night
or how I pushed a lemon seed into soil four summers ago
and now have shade—
that once in a while I can almost see her dolled up and laughing
again, serving up cocktails and beef bourguignon to the neighbors,
trusting my tiny hands to carry out the tray of hors d'oeuvres.
How I loved her long velvet skirts and silk blouses,
especially the one with giant polka dots, or
when we saw *Schindler's List* and cried over Carvel
on the way home.
She doesn't remember we spoke yesterday
but still tears up over the little girl in the red coat. I want to tell her
that the little girl in the red coat is now 32 and lives in Krakow,
helping Ukrainian refugees cross the border.
I want to tell her so many things:
about each ex-lover tattooed on my insides—
two stolen pint glasses and a hike through the snow, hunks
of peach pie at a road stand in summer, an icy graveyard in Paris.
How the pipes in my walk-up on Jane Street hissed like her anger,
and how like a cloudy lens behind the iris is this sliver of
pinkish root. I want to ask her if, along with the highway
and her watercolors, she will see me more clearly come fall.

Rocks

Once my father took me for a ride in his Buick to the lumberyard.
He heaved a bag of sand up across his shoulder and slugged it
down on the counter.

I thought I'd never seen such strength and ran my hands
through the bins of nails and screws underneath.

We were shy with each other: at the sandbox, all week,
he with his briefcase on trains, me waiting for a glimpse of him.

Another Saturday he took me to the creek down by the church—

helped me choose rocks for my collection, splintered off a fleck of
mica the color of molten steel. He placed it in my hand as though a
moth wing

before I knew of words like

ephemeral   or
                           gentle father

Even then I knew this couldn't last.
I was a flimsy stand-in for yellow legal pads, 5:30 Mass, my
brother's ghost. I wished I was a boy.

I still search backroads for streams.
Their wet, mossy rocks and ferns, gritty bottoms.
I still feel my cheeks for beard.

Prayer

Sometimes I'll picture Julia Roberts asking God to show his face
in *Eat Pray Love,* twisting bed sheets into ribbon candy.
Or close my eyes and imagine hands grasping for air;
folded, dirty, desperate—for potatoes
(as in Jean-François Millet's *The Angelus*)—
like Grandma's, wrapped around an ax,
chopping down blue spruce for cash each Christmas.
Each summer, she'd wait for us at the Greyhound station,
then weave us through forest in her rusty blue Nova
to her house full of holes and torn wallpaper.
I'd run wild through the creek and long grasses
tangled with cornsilk and gooseberry vines,
swallow fists of pansies and dirt as the sky purpled.
She'd put the Oak Ridge Boys on her turntable,
or *Hee Haw* on TV. We'd feast on tomato sandwiches
and beans snapped fresh off the stalk.
When she winked and snuck me a swig of moonshine,
I knew she must be a saint. I'd curl my hands into hers
and whisper thanks for those hills of summer,
the smell of ginger snaps in the oven,
her blue gingham dress.

To New Paltz

On the road to New Paltz we drink the air
that rushes in from 287 and stuff our mouths
with sandwiches from the deli that seconds
as a drum shop.

You squeal when Bowie comes on the mix I made,
and between you squeezing my hand
and the sign for New York,
I'm a kid pinned in blue ribbons.

You point out the mountains ahead, swear
we will hike them, swim like fish in their lake.
In town we buy falafels and notebooks—
you lose me, I find you

barefoot against a cracking wall.
We sit by the river,
unbox our new compass. You point it North,
tell me a story of being lost in the woods.

We kiss hard, and I promise
you will never lose your way again,
that between me and the compass
it's impossible.

Driving home, we are weary—
the mountains and lake shrink behind us,
taillights smudge the rear window red
as treacherous embankments flash by—

I press my forehead against the glass,
wonder if some promises can't be kept,
what they would look like
smashed on the rocks below.

At the Lake

that final Sunday of summer, you snuck us past the *Members Only*
sign to the line of canoes tied up and bobbing against the dock.

We exhaled and kissed with the arrogance of thieves, dipped our
feet in the circling minnows. We dove off the edge to the rocky

bottom, dove into each other, as the last carload left the parking
lot; your skin tasted like melon and the air after rain. You sucked

the knob of my shoulder and the breath from my lungs—when
your hands touched my thighs, I could have walked on water.

As the sun slid behind the houses on the opposite shore, we
watched the sky turn the shade of blackberries and blue smoke

of barbecues. We laughed and swore to love, to forever,
swore to keep swimming straight into fall,

straight through the deep end—drowning out
the cold ache of dusk and any dangers ahead.

Fireworks

The fireworks go off in Asbury Park,
perfectly timed to another hot flash, another pill,
startling me as though I were right there on the boardwalk,

though I have not yet returned—like everything else we shared
still too hot to touch.

I can't tell what's worse, losing my insides or us. Your hands
keep appearing in my dreams of wrong trains and crying babies,
silver-ringed half-moons orbiting mine.

This mattress sags from grief

as I trace the surgeon's handiwork
and wonder how long before the raw red lines
fade to scars,

if parts left behind
shift into the void,

why we can still see the fireworks
after they explode.

Ash Wednesday

I keep finding you today:
in the line of souls waiting for their ashes
       under the church bell's heavy toll,

the seagull circling and searching for others, miles lost
from our old shore,
here on the coffee table:

       that photo of you doing your best Bowie,
       our book of Mary Karr,
       the compass we bought one summer—

if we had used it more precisely,

       could we have finally found each other

       could it have pointed me toward you that March night

in time to save you from your sins, save me from my own,

spare the rest of us from having to scatter you
among the rocks and pines of your mountain,

       as if to fall to our knees and atone

       as if to blacken our foreheads with your name

Things We Did on the Internet

She found me on the internet when I wasn't looking.
Posed a random question, innocuous, with just enough flirt to
laugh about later.

Once, I texted her a song about astronauts, then taught her how to
download it. She played me Patti Smith, who sang of shy, tattooed
fingers and a river.

For a while, we pinned photos to our online corkboards; she fell in
love again with Twiggy's hair, and I made a collage of orange.

We searched Maps for old places—
the deli where her grandma bought cold cuts, the hill where mine
grew potatoes.

One night in bed, I read her Frank O'Hara from my phone,
and she whispered me her favorite word: *perspicacious.*

"Sagacious, astute," spoke the Dictionary, once she'd fallen asleep.
If only, I think now.

If only our so-called wisdom could swoop in through soft-green
curtains to save someone.

If only I could type out, *What happens to a body that swallows too
many pills?* then bring myself to read all the piss and shit of it.

If only you could download every single gigabyte of your guts,
hand her the flash drive, and convince her to stay.

Afternoon Storm

Thunder cracks, angry rain
pounds clean her new marigolds
and scrubs winter's grime from the stoop.

She blusters back out for the avocado
while I stay behind to empty our bags,
figure out what else we may have forgotten.

I pull a knife from the drawer
and sink it into the tomato's flesh,
let it bleed into the cutting board's
old nicks and slivers—just the tiniest traces
of me here at her place.

She smacks the screen door back open,
ripe fruit in hand, electricity flickers.
I wonder which way this storm might blow,
if I should have run while I had the chance.

Arrowhead

My dead are scattered:
forest in elk country, sleeve of island off the city,
graveyard filled with stars.
In the shadow of boulders on a mountain—she and I
hiked there each Sunday morning like church. Climbing, climbing
we would pause to catch our breath, pick up a feather or rock,
kiss like we were starving—her tongue tasting of granola and pine.
Foolish thief, I pocketed the arrowhead we discovered one fall.
How could I have known the cost of stealing from the dead?
That the mountain would demand something in return:
the violence of pills, her body in ash.

The First Time

We met halfway in late afternoon
at a motel off the interstate.
The shadows of clouds floated past us
in the pool; we circled each other,
a pair of awkward birds. I tried
showing off, suddenly a teenage boy,
swimming from one side to the other.
At dinner we shared the two for one
special and a slice of pie. I bought
a postcard in the gift shop. Later
we lay entwined without sheets. Our
sweaty skin made a sucking sound
when we tried to shift apart. I licked the curve
of your neck. Your hair smelled of cinnamon.
In the hall, someone pulled the fire alarm.
We scrambled to put on whatever clothes
we could find on the floor, laughing
at the implausibility of it all.
Outside, we waited for directions.
You wrapped your sweater around me.

Visiting Fellowship

Your father wakes at dawn to pick the blueberries,
Mississippi sun rising cruel and mean

as a seventies summer in the city.
An old rifle stands in the corner, two southern flags

folded in triangles perch on a shelf. I wonder
what he thinks of me, this girl from the north,

this lover of his daughter. He returns through the screen
with three bagsful to dump and wash in the sink,

purple-fisted and proud as though he's just won a war.
We walk with your mother up the road before breakfast,

past the grassed-over graves of soldiers and a giant magnolia.
You point out a mockingbird, but I've got my eyes peeled

for hanging ghosts and rattlesnakes—I can't wait to get back
inside. The four of us hold hands as your father blesses

the pancakes, and for one sweet moment, loving you here
in this kitchen, I swallow enough shame for all of us.

Breakfast

You slip from our sheets to make coffee
and feed the cats. Slice open the peaches
we bought yesterday at the farm,
fist a lump of dough into circles.
Sun slides through blue mountains and the curtain of trees,
lands on my thigh. I could lie here forever
feigning sleep just to peek at you through the door.
You tiptoe to your piano and play Mozart
so softly I can barely hear.
I lose sight of your hands and am ravenous—
I've hungered for such kindness,
breath that comes so easily.
The only eggshells here in this cabin
the ones you leave cracked in the bowl.

Playing Detectives

What do I know of love, sister,
but long-distance and suicide

(my heart is just a hunk of blood and gristle,
beating quicker than others its size just to keep up, doctors tell me).

We used to play detectives in summer's dusk,
sneaking like cats around the cars

in the boardwalk parking garage,
doing our best *Hart to Hart*

long before you caught his eye, before he tossed you
like scraps in the yard,

else I would have signaled to you
and snuck up on him,

pointed my loaded cap gun to his heart and pulled.

Giant

My father is shrinking.
His head sinks into his chest as he slowly rises
from his armchair to say goodbye.
That look on his face
when my mother snaps, *Stand up, Jim.*
This old man's rages stifled
could set fire to forests, given half a chance.
One Saturday evening in winter, he drove us
home after Mass, swerving through snow,
my sister and I smart enough to stay silent in the backseat.
His silver-haired head giant in the shadowy glow
of passing street lights, his hands steering us to safety.
Tonight, I wonder if he longed to reach over to touch the nape of
her neck. I wonder tonight if he would have preferred to drop us
off, then disappear. My father is disappearing.
An empty navy-blue sweater
I try to grip onto a bit longer before leaving.

Insomnia

Forests are choking tonight,
fox and cicadas cry in the smoke.

I count my sins and say a Hail Mary,
reach for the still-unread mystery borrowed from Dad.

Loud sirens race down Route 35
and give me strange comfort. I wonder

if he hears them too, though I know
he is too far away. I wonder

where his mind goes on sleepless nights,
if insomnia returns his beloved rituals:

jumping into the Hudson as a boy in summer,
pulling work from his briefcase on trains

to the city and trains back home.
Counting his pennies. Counting birds. Counting cars on the road.

I picture filling bags for the Goodwill
with old suits and swim trunks,

manila folders and papers,
everything we have yet to give each other;

my father padding through darkness
to the kitchen, filling a glass of water from the sink,

his throat on fire like mine,
burning, with everything we have yet to say.

Salvage

Laura's mother has died in the night—
she tells me there is nothing I can do

but say a prayer and check in on the dogs,
who want feeding and a run around the yard.

I'm not sure I know how to pray anymore
so I sweep the kitchen. The strawberries have turned

but I wash them anyway, rubbing each one under water.
I am no monster, I always salvage what I can—

coffee grounds and the fly caught behind the pane.
I could not spare my brother the fever that winter

nor my father the bones that betray him now;
Leslie would have found the bottles wherever I hid them,

under the sink or the pines out back—
all this grief could burn us alive.

My marigolds have scorched in the sun
so I pluck each seed from its burnt plume;

I should save them in an envelope to plant next spring
but push them back into soil, mix in the rotting bits of berry.

Dead Things

I feel compelled to pick up the baby bird that has died
just outside my doorstep this morning. Place her in my hand
and rub her toothpick ribs with my thumb, pull the lids down
over the milky-blue bulbs of her eyes. Yesterday I drove to the city
through rain and came upon a deer lying bent in the road.
How then I wished to pull over and push my fist into her wounds,
sift through her insides as though they were the yellowing
ephemera I've shoved deep into closets. In front of the theater on
Broadway, a man lay still and drenched. How easy it would have
been to give him a coffee, hold his hand, check for life.
Now here, in this morning's fog, I see I have stood too long again.
Cherry blossom snow wilts on the cement and the ants
surround the tiny carcass. They stumble and march onward,
heft the weight of what remains onto their backs.

Lines for Self

Tell yourself
as the moon turns scarlet and the morning tides pull you closer
that you will keep walking these sands, same as you always have—
that your feet are not weary, that the lines on your hands are not
there, the strand of silver in your brush is a fluke.
Tonight, in the suffocating air of a dying spring,
you are sucking down moonshine on Grandma's back porch
and smoking corn-silk cigarettes on her tire swing.
You are rambling toward your third-floor walk-up
and happy to be lost in this city at 3 a.m.
You are with your new lover in a bathroom stall
and watching the sun rise from her favorite mountain.
You tell yourself, yes, all of it did just happen yesterday—
and you believe the lie. Tomorrow
you can think back to colder nights when you saw the cruelty of
stars and curl yourself under their blanket. Stretch yourself out
on that sleeve of rocks where you once splashed. Tell yourself
you have loved and been loved, rest easy.

About the Author

Originally from Westchester County in New York, Beth Boylan now lives and writes near the ocean in New Jersey. She earned an MA in Literature from Hunter College. Beth's work has been nominated for a Pushcart Prize and Best of the Net and appears in a variety of journals, including *Rust + Moth, New York Quarterly, The McNeese Review, Birdcoat Quarterly, Nixes Mate Review, Whale Road Review,* and *Peatsmoke.*

www.ingramcontent.com/pod-product-compliance
Lightning Source LLC
Chambersburg PA
CBHW070906100426
42737CB00047B/2973